Before I Was Born

God Knew My Name

CAROLYN NYSTROM

A NavPress resource published in alliance
with Tyndale House Publishers, Inc.

NavPress is the publishing ministry of The Navigators, an international Christian organization and leader in personal spiritual development. NavPress is committed to helping people grow spiritually and enjoy lives of meaning and hope through personal and group resources that are biblically rooted, culturally relevant, and highly practical.

For more information, visit www.NavPress.com.

Before I Was Born: God Knew My Name

Copyright © 1983, 1995, 2007, 2019 by Carolyn Nystrom. All rights reserved.

A NavPress resource published in alliance with Tyndale House Publishers, Inc.

NAVPRESS is a registered trademark of NavPress, The Navigators, Colorado Springs, CO. The NAVPRESS logo is a trademark of NavPress, The Navigators. *TYNDALE* is a registered trademark of Tyndale House Publishers, Inc. Absence of ® in connection with marks of NavPress or other parties does not indicate an absence of registration of those marks.

The Team for the Third Edition:

Don Pape, Publisher
Caitlyn Carlson, Developmental Editor
Jennifer Ghionzoli, Designer
Sandra Speidel, Illustrator
Text from original Crossway edition, copyright 1983.

Cover and interior illustrations of birds, bees, and vine copyright © mightyisland/Getty Images. All rights reserved.

Scripture quotations are taken from *The Holy Bible*, English Standard Version® (ESV®), copyright © 2001 by Crossway, a publishing ministry of Good News Publishers. Used by permission. All rights reserved.

For information about special discounts for bulk purchases, please contact Tyndale House Publishers at csresponse@tyndale.com, or call 1-800-323-9400.

Cataloging-in-Publication Data is available.

ISBN 978-1-64158-145-5

Printed in China

27   26   25   24   23
7   6   5   4   3

AN IMPORTANT WORD TO PARENTS

General Introduction to the God's Design for Sex Series

BY STAN & BRENNA JONES

PARENTS, GOD GAVE YOU your sexuality as a precious gift. And you're reading this book because God has given you a child you love as a gift flowing from your sexuality.

God gave your child the gift of sexuality as well. If handled responsibly, this gift will be a source of blessing and delight. How can parents help make this happen?

Many forces will push children to make bad choices about sex based on false beliefs and values and on misplaced spiritual priorities. These forces are more powerful, confusing, persuasive, and ever present today than ever in history, thanks to the power of social media and the confusion of our culture. From their earliest years, children are bombarded with destructive, misleading messages—messages about the nature of sexual intimacy, about marriage, about family, about the boundaries of godly sexual expression, and even about the basic creational design of humanity as male and female.

These messages come from everywhere—through music, television, the Internet, discussions with their friends, school sex-education programs, and many other sources. The result? Confusion, doubt, and shame, as well as distressing rates of sexual experimentation, teen pregnancy, abortion, sexually transmitted disease, divorce, and devastated lives.

We believe that *God means for Christian parents to be their children's primary sex educators.* First messages are the most powerful—why wait until your child hears distorted views and then try to correct the misunderstanding? Sexuality is a beautiful gift—why not present it to your child the way God intended? God's Word is trustworthy and true—why not teach your child how to understand and live by its guidance in the area of sexuality? Why not establish yourself as the trusted expert to whom your child can turn to hear God's truth about sexuality?

The God's Design for Sex series is designed to help parents shape their children's character, particularly in the area of sexuality. Sex education in the family is less about giving biological information and more about *shaping your child's moral character.* The earlier you start helping your child see himself or herself as God does, including in the area of sexuality, the stronger your child will be as they enter the turbulent teenage years.

How and When to Tell Your Kids about Sex is a parents' resource manual in which we offer a comprehensive understanding of what parents can do to shape their children's sexual character. The four children's books in this series are designed for parents and children to work through together. Those books are structured to be read with your child at ages three to five (*The Story of Me*), five to eight (*Before I Was Born*), eight to twelve (*What's the Big Deal?*), and twelve to sixteen (*Facing the Facts*). These age ranges are not strict formulas; you need to exercise your judgment about your child's maturity level, environment, needs, and so forth to decide when and how to introduce the books.

The four children's books are meant to provide the foundational information kids need. Further, they are to be starting points for you to build upon and personalize as you discuss sexuality with your child in an age-appropriate manner. They provide an anchor point for discussions in order to jump-start deeper explorations. These books help break the silence and put the issues out on the table.

Don't simply hand these books to your child to read, *because our whole point is to empower you as the parent to shape your child's sexual character.* The books are meant to start and shape conversations between you and your child and to deepen your impact on your child in the area of sexuality.

In this series, we address controversial topics about which Christians disagree, including masturbation, how far people should go sexually when they're dating, contraception, gender identity, homosexuality, and more. Our goal in doing so is not to presumptuously present our answers as completely right but rather to encourage you to reach reasoned conclusions and to teach your child as you see fit before the Lord.

We have tried in each book to present information that we believe children of that age must have, without presenting controversial topics "too early." Your child may be confronted with complicated and confusing issues at a much earlier age than you expect. In such cases, you can draw on our discussions in later books to inform your dialogue with your child. For instance, we hold off on discussion of sexual orientation until the book for eight-to-twelve-year-olds (*What's the Big Deal?*), and on discussion of gender identity and transgender issues until the book for twelve-to-sixteen-year-olds (*Facing the Facts*). But your child may need more basic information much earlier, and in such cases, we urge you to use or adapt material from this book and our books for older children to meet your child's needs.

Why start early? Because if you as the parent are not teaching your child about sexuality, your child will learn distorted lessons about sexuality from television, the Internet, and playground conversations. If you are silent on sex while the rest of the world is abuzz about it, your child will learn that you cannot help in this key area. If you teach godly, truthful, tactful, and appropriate lessons about sexuality, your child will trust you more and see you as a parent who tells the truth.

We'll briefly unpack each of the books at more length to help you discern which would be most helpful to you in your current parenting season.

How and When to Tell Your Kids about Sex:

A Lifelong Approach to Shaping Your Child's Sexual Character

This book is the parents' comprehensive resource manual for the God's Design for Sex series. We take on the hardest subjects, such as sexual abuse, gender identity, and homosexuality, helping you know when and how to bring up these subjects. Our goals for *How and When to Tell Your Kids about Sex* are to

- **HELP** you understand your role in shaping your child's character, including his or her views, attitudes, and beliefs about sexuality;

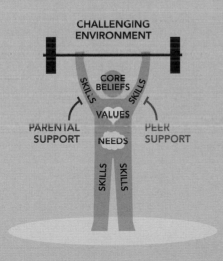

CHALLENGING
ENVIRONMENT

CORE
BELIEFS
SKILLS   SKILLS
VALUES
PARENTAL   PEER
SUPPORT   SUPPORT
NEEDS
SKILLS   SKILLS

- **INSTRUCT** you in the twelve key principles for Christian sex education in the home and how to implement the strategies and tactics suggested by these principles;

- **FAMILIARIZE** you with the challenges that your child will face from secular culture and empower you with strategies and skills to help them overcome those challenges;

- **GROUND** your understanding of God's view of our sexuality;

- **EQUIP** you and your child to explain and defend the traditional Christian view of sexual morality in these modern times;

- **EXAMINE** each major developmental stage of your child's life and share age-appropriate information and approaches;

- **ADDRESS** directly the most complex issues you and your child might or will face in today's culture in a manner grounded in biblical thinking and informed by the best contemporary science;

- **EXPLORE** how you can most powerfully influence your child to live a life of sexual chastity; and

- **EQUIP** you to provide your child with the strengths necessary to stand by their commitment to traditional Christian morality.

As you read the following descriptions of each of the books for your child, please know that the concepts and issues presented in each of these books flow directly from the background provided by this foundational parents' guide.

Ages Three to Five

The Story of Me: *Babies, Bodies, and a Very Good God*

Your most important task with your young child is to lay a spiritual foundation for their understanding of sexuality. God loves the human body (and the whole human person), and the body is included in what God called "very good" (Genesis 1:31). Children's bodies, their existence as boys or girls, and also their sexual organs are gifts from God.

Young children can begin to develop a wondrous appreciation for God's marvelous gift of sexuality by understanding some of the basics of fetal development. In this book, we discuss the growth of a child inside a mother's body and the birth process. With such instruction, young children begin to develop a trust for God's law and to see God as a lawgiver who has the best interests of his people at heart. God is the giver of good gifts!

Finally, we want children to see families grounded on the lifelong marital union of one man and one woman as God's intended framework for the nurture and love of children. If you are reading the book as a single parent or with an adopted child, you will have opportunity to talk about how God sometimes creates and blesses alternative forms of families. We hope that you will find *The Story of Me* a wonderful starting point for discussing sexuality with your young child.

Ages Five to Eight

Before I Was Born: *God Knew My Name*
by Carolyn Nystrom, with Stan and Brenna Jones

Before I Was Born emphasizes the creational goodness of our bodies, our existence as men and women, and our sexual organs. This book introduces new topics as well, including the growth and changes boys and girls experience as they become men and women.

It includes a tactful but direct explanation of sexual intercourse between husbands and wives. God wants sexual intercourse limited to marriage, because sexual intercourse brings husbands and wives close together in a way that honors God and helps to build strong families.

Parents often ask, "Do my kids really need to know about sexual intercourse this early?" Remembering that you are the decision maker as to whether you use this book with a very mature five-year-old or with a more slowly maturing eight-year-old, the answer is yes. We believe this is a strategic decision parents must face based on their individual children, considering that first messages are always the most powerful messages. If, as a Christian parent, you want to begin to shape a godly attitude in your child about sex, why would you wait until they first soak in the misperceptions of the world? Why not build godly attitudes and views from the foundation up?

If you're reading this with an adopted child, use this opportunity to explain that not every couple will have biological children. If a baby doesn't grow in the wife's womb, the couple might look for a baby to adopt. And some women are not able to take care of a baby, so another family might adopt the baby and make it part of their family forever. Even though the baby grew inside a different mother, the husband and wife love this baby very much. Adoption is another way that God makes families.

Ages Eight to Twelve
What's the Big Deal?: Why God Cares about Sex

This book reinforces the messages of our first two children's books, covering the basics of sexual intercourse and the fundamental creational goodness of our sexuality. It continues the task of deliberately building children's understanding of why God intends sexual intercourse to be reserved for marriage.

This book goes further than the earlier books, adding more of the facts your child will need to know as they approach puberty. Further, it will help you begin the process of inoculating your child against the negative moral messages of the world. In *How and When to Tell Your Kids about Sex*, we argue that Christian parents should *not* try to completely shelter their children from the destructive moral messages of the world. If they mature in environments where they are not exposed to germs, children grow up with depleted immune systems that are ineffectual for resisting disease. When parents shelter their children too much, children are left naive and vulnerable; parents risk communicating that the negative messages of the world are so powerful that Christians cannot even talk about them.

But neither should you let your child be inundated with society's destructive messages. The principle of inoculation suggests that you should deliberately expose your child to the contrary moral messages they will hear from the world. It should be in your *home* that your child first learns that many people in our world do not believe in reserving sex for marriage, and it should be in your home that your child first understands such problems as pornography, teenage pregnancy, gay marriage, sexual identity and gender issues, and so forth. In this way, you can help build your child's defenses against departing from God's ways.

Ages Twelve to Sixteen

Facing the Facts: The Truth about Sex and You

Facing the Facts: The Truth about Sex and You builds upon all that has come before but also—in more depth—prepares your child for puberty. At this age, your child is old enough for more detailed information about the changes their body is about to go through and about the adult body they will soon receive as a gift from God.

In this book, your child will hear again about God's view of sexuality and about his loving and beautiful intentions for how this gift should be used. The distorted ways in which our world views sex must be clearly labeled, and your child must be prepared to face views and beliefs contrary to those they learn at home. We attempt to do all this while also talking about the many confusing feelings of puberty and early adolescence.

While children could read this book independently, we do not believe this would be optimal. We encourage you to read it alongside your child and then talk about it together. You could go chapter by chapter. Alternatively, you can read it and use it as a resource for important conversations with your soon-to-be or young teenager.

In this book, we address the most controversial topics of the series, topics about which biblically grounded Christians can and do frequently disagree. We make suggestions about appropriate moral positions on all of the important issues, including sexual-intimacy limits before marriage, masturbation, contraception, gender identity, homosexuality, and more.

We have joked that in each of these books, we are guaranteed to say something to lead almost any Christian parent to declare us too conservative or too liberal on some topic or to disagree with us somewhere. We do not presume our answers are completely right. At the very least, we hope our thoughts empower you, the parent, to think the matter through and present a better answer to your child as the Lord guides your thinking.

All of these books were written as if dialogue is an ongoing reality between mother, father, and child. Yet in some homes, only one parent is willing to talk about sex. Many Christian parents shoulder the responsibility of parenting alone due to separation, divorce, or death. Grandparents sometimes must raise their grandkids. We've tried to be sensitive to adoptive families and families that do not fit the mold of the traditional nuclear family, but we cannot anticipate or respond to all the unique needs of families. Use these books with creativity and discernment to meet the needs of your situation.

We hope these books will be valuable tools in raising a new generation of faithful Christian young people. If you follow this plan, we believe your child will have a healthy, positive, accepting, godly attitude about sexuality. As an unmarried person, your child will be more likely to live a confident, chaste life as a faithful witness to the work of Christ in their heart. If your child does marry, we believe they will have a greater chance of having a fulfilled, loving, rewarding life as a husband or wife. It is our prayer that this curriculum will encourage and equip you to dive into the wonderful work of shaping your child's sexual character.

CAROLYN NYSTROM began her career as a teacher of second graders in a public school. After several years, she then took a "mom break." She and her husband, Roger (also a teacher), parented the two daughters born to them, along with providing temporary care for five foster children—two eventually adopted into their family. As a homemaker mom (including a special needs child) Carolyn began a second career as a writer, resulting in several dozen Bible study guides and children's books, including *What Happens When We Die?*, winner of the ECPA Gold Medallion Award for children's books. Later she coauthored several books with historian Mark Noll and also with theologian J. I. Packer.

Carolyn has served as an elder in her church, as stated clerk of Rivers and Lakes Presbytery of the Evangelical Presbyterian Church, and later as caregiver for her husband. When possible she enjoys hiking and camping in national parks. She holds a master's degree in historical theology from Wheaton College.

STAN (STANTON L.) JONES, PHD, is a clinical psychologist. He recently returned to serving as professor of psychology at Wheaton College after serving for twenty years as its provost (chief academic officer). Earlier, he led in establishing Wheaton's PsyD program in clinical psychology. He has been a visiting scholar at the University of Cambridge and has published many articles in journals such as *American Psychologist, General Psychologist, First Things,* and *Christianity Today.* Beyond the God's Design for Sex series, his books include *Psychology: A Student's Guide, Modern Psychotherapies: A Comprehensive Christian Appraisal* (2nd ed., with Richard E. Butman), *Ex-Gays?: A Longitudinal Study of Religiously Mediated Change in Sexual Orientation* (with Mark A. Yarhouse), and *Homosexuality: The Use of Scientific Research in the Church's Moral Debate* (with Mark A. Yarhouse).

BRENNA JONES serves in a professional ministry of discipleship and support as well as spiritual counsel and prayer for women. She served as a leader in a Bible-study ministry with women for a number of years. She has graduate training in biblical and theological studies.

BRENNA & STAN wrote the original versions of their books on sex education while their three children were young; now they enjoy their three kids as adults, along with their kids' spouses and children.

LONG AGO, before there was moon or sun or stars or anything else, there was God.

God knew you. And he loved you—even then.

What color is your hair?

Are your eyes blue or brown or green?

Are you quiet and shy or full of silly giggles?

Before God made the world, he thought about you.

He even knew your name.

God made the sky and the ground and the rivers and the oceans.

He made huge animals and tiny bugs and wind and rain.

He made grass and flowers and trees.

He made bright blue-sky days,

and he made splashy rain days.

Then God looked at everything he had made.

He said, "It is all good."

But God wasn't finished.

God said, "Let's make a man and a woman in our image." And he did!

God looked at the bare bodies of the two people he had made. He saw the man's scratchy beard and the woman's soft breasts, and he was glad. He said, "I made their bodies wonderful. They are both like me.

"And they will love each other and join their lives together as one."

When a new baby is born, parents and grandparents and friends are happy and proud.

One of the first things they brag is

"It's a boy!"

or

"It's a girl!"

What did they all say when you were born?

A boy baby has a penis and a scrotum between his legs. The scrotum is a soft bag that holds two round hard organs called testicles. His penis is soft and spongy, and it sticks out a bit from his body. When the baby gets older, he can stand up while he passes urine from the opening at the tip of his penis. Sometimes his penis gets hard and stiff for a few minutes, but most of the time it stays soft and close to his body. God made these parts of a boy so that someday, when he is a man, he and his wife can make a baby.

Boy babies grow to be little boys. They learn to run and climb and read. Their bodies are bigger than when they were babies, but they are still boy bodies.

Girl babies grow to be little girls. They learn to run and climb and read too. A girl has three openings close together between her legs. A girl passes urine through the front opening, but she sits down to do this. From the back opening she passes bowel movements, just like a boy does.

The opening in the middle is her vagina. It is a small narrow tunnel that leads up to her womb and then to two ovaries inside her body. God made a girl's ovaries so that they hold tiny eggs. But while she is a little girl, her tiny eggs stay safe inside her ovaries. When she is a grown-up and ready to become a mother, an egg can become a baby and grow inside her womb. But how?

Little boys do not stay little boys. A boy gets bigger and bigger as he begins to look like a man. His shoulders grow wide. His arm muscles grow more thick. His voice gets deep, and his whole body gets more hairy. He grows hair under his arms and above his penis, and maybe on his chest. He may even grow a beard.

A boy's penis gets larger too. His two testicles make millions of tiny sperm too small to see, and the sperm stay inside his scrotum. When the boy is ready to be a dad, his body will add the sperm to a fluid called semen. Semen can help a husband make a baby with his wife.

A girl's body changes too. She grows hair under her arms and above her vagina. She grows taller. Her hips grow fuller. She develops two soft breasts on her chest.

The inside of her body changes too. Once a month her womb gets thick and soft. Then a tiny egg no bigger than a dot moves from an ovary to her womb and then out through her vagina. Her body is getting ready to take care of a baby. But she is not a mother yet.

Do you ever wonder what your grown-up body will look like?

God planned for men and women to love each other. That's why he made one man and one woman in the beginning. When a man and a woman love each other for some time, they think about getting married. Being married is God's way of giving a person one certain friend all of the time. But men and women need to choose carefully whom they will marry. After they are married, God wants them to stay together as long as they both live.

A wedding is a happy time! The man and woman stand in front of their family and friends. They invite God and everyone there to listen to their promises. They promise to love and take care of each other as long as they both live.

At the end the pastor says, "I now pronounce you husband and wife. What God has joined, let no one take apart." Everyone smiles because God has made a new family.

Friends bring gifts to a wedding. God also made a special gift for husbands and wives. It is called sex. God's rules say that only people who are married to each other should have sex. It is God's way of making families strong.

After a man and woman are married, they share their bodies with each other. They like holding each other close. When a husband and a wife lie close together, he can fit his penis into her vagina. His semen flows inside of her, and their bodies feel good all over. Husbands and wives want to be alone during sex so they can think only of each other.

This is the way babies are made. A husband can't make a baby by himself. A wife can't make a baby by herself. But God made their bodies to fit perfectly together. And together they can make a baby.

A husband and wife don't make a baby every time they have sex. But sometimes the sperm in the semen from the husband's penis comes into his wife just when an egg from her body is ready to receive it. Then the sperm joins the egg and they become one new cell—no bigger than the period at the end of this sentence. Did you know that you were once that tiny?

A baby is already beginning to grow—inside its mother's womb. If you could see inside that tiny, tiny cell, you could know whether the baby will have blue eyes or brown. You could tell whether it will have dark or light hair. You could tell whether it will be a boy or a girl. You could even tell how tall it will be when it is all grown up. The baby will look a little like its mother and a little like its father because it is made from both of them. But the baby isn't ready to be born. Not yet.

The womb is a wonderful place inside a mother's body. At first the womb is no bigger than your fist.

Can you find the baby inside the mother in the picture? By the time the baby has been living in the womb for three months, it looks like this. Sometimes the baby holds its hands together as if to play "patty-cake." It might even suck its thumb.

The baby is only as long as your finger. A long umbilical cord connects the baby with the inside of the womb.

The mother's tummy isn't much bigger than it was before. Some people don't even know that she is going to have a baby. But she knows.

The baby isn't ready to be born. Not yet.

As the baby grows, the womb stretches until it is as big as a watermelon.

By the time a baby has been living in the womb for six months, it has hair and fingernails and eyelashes, and it is nearly twelve inches long. But the baby doesn't breathe yet. It gets all the air and food it needs through the cord. At lunchtime the baby's mom might pat her belly and say to a friend, "I'm eating for two now."

The growing baby can hear the mother's heartbeat, breathing, and voice. It can even hear some sounds outside the mother's body. If you talk next to a pregnant mother's belly, the baby inside may hear you!

Sometimes the baby kicks and stretches. The mother smiles when she feels this. She knows her baby is getting stronger. Because the mother's tummy is getting bigger, everyone knows that she is going to have a baby. They say, "She's pregnant."

But the baby isn't ready to be born. Not yet.

When the baby has been living in the womb for eight months, it is almost as big as a newborn baby. It gets ready to eat by sucking its thumb. It gets ready to breathe by moving its chest up and down. It gets ready to move around by kicking hard.

The mother is tired a lot, but she is excited, too. She knows that soon she will see her baby. The father stays close to home. If he has to go away, he takes his phone so the mother can call him. He knows their baby will be born soon, and he doesn't want to miss it.

Finally, after about nine months, the big day comes. The womb that has stretched and stretched now begins to get smaller. Slowly it pushes the baby out. The baby moves down, headfirst, closer to the mother's vagina.

The mother feels her womb muscles push hard. She feels her vagina stretch open. It hurts, and it is hard work. Her husband stays with her to help her not to be afraid. A doctor or nurse helps too. It takes a long time for a baby to be born—maybe a whole day.

Finally, the baby's head squeezes out from the mother's vagina. The baby's whole body follows quickly. The new baby takes a deep breath and begins to cry.

The doctor says, "It's a boy!" or "It's a girl!"

How do you think the doctor knows?

The doctor cuts the baby's cord. It doesn't hurt.
The baby won't need the cord anymore. Later he will
have a belly button to show where the cord fastened
him to his mother.

The mother holds her baby. Soon he stops crying
and sucks happily at her breast. God made the womb
a wonderful place for the baby to grow before he is born.
God also made the woman's breasts just right for giving
the baby milk after he is born.

The mother and father laugh and hug each other.
The pain is gone. The mother strokes her baby's hair.
The father puts a finger into the baby's tiny hand. This
is one of the happiest moments of their lives. They
thank God for their baby.

Long ago, before the world was made, God planned for this
moment. God planned that this baby would be formed partly
from his mother and partly from his father. God helped their
baby grow for nine months inside his mother's womb.
God planned his hair and his eyes and his whole
body. God even knew his name. And God planned
that he would be born—that he would live
and breathe. And by God's plan, like
every other human baby that has
been born, he is made in the
image of God.

God planned you, too. And he has given you a wonderful body. Have you thanked him for it?

God made every one of us, whether we marry or stay single, to be an image or picture of himself, just like the first man and woman.

When a man and a woman become husband and wife, God gives them the blessing of sharing their bodies with each other. When their love creates a new baby, they together can show the whole world a new and different picture of God.

God took special delight in creating human beings. He loves us, and we are *his* children. Each one of us, and each new family we form, can become a beautiful picture of God.

How does the love in your family remind you of God? Have you thanked God for your family?

For you formed my inward parts;

you knitted me together in my mother's womb.

I praise you, for I am fearfully and wonderfully made.

Wonderful are your works;

my soul knows it very well.

My frame was not hidden from you,

when I was being made in secret,

intricately woven.

PSALM 139:13–15